the SCOTTISH GUITAR

40 Scottish Tunes for Fingerstyle Guitar

by Rob MacKillop

*This book and the recording are dedicated
to my accordion/saxophone-playing father.*

ISBN 978-1-57424-265-2
SAN 683-8022

Cover by James Creative Group

Copyright © 2011 CENTERSTREAM Publishing, LLC
P.O. Box 17878 - Anaheim Hills, CA 92817

www.centerstream-usa.com

CONTENTS & CD Track List

About the Author

Rob MacKillop is a composer, researcher, performer and recording artist who has for many years specialised in the historical Scottish music for lutes and guitars. He also plays the classic banjo and ukulele. He was awarded a Churchill Fellowship to study with Sufi musicians in Istanbul and Morocco, and has recorded for Greentrax, ASV Gaudeamus, Dorian, Alpha and other labels. Rob has publications with Mel Bay in the USA, and The Hardie Press in the UK. He has conducted many workshops and masterclasses at international festivals and local schools.

Reviews

'One of Scotland's finest musicians' - *Celtic World*

'A top-drawer player' - *Early Music Today*

'A true champion of Scottish music' - *The Herald*

'A player of real quality, with warmth of personality and communication skills to match...one of Scotland's top professionals' - *Classical Guitar*

'MacKillop displays dazzling virtuosity...the playing is exceptionally musical' - *Sounding Strings*

'a leading traditional talent who is single-handedly responsible for unearthing some of the nation's finest music' - *The Scotsman*

Website: www.RMguitar.info

About the Recording

I made the recording at Pier House Studios in Edinburgh, with Peter Haigh at the desk. Two mics (AKG and Neumann) were placed about two feet away, slightly to my right. The mics fed straight into a computer where a subtle level of reverb was added. Each track is a complete take. I performed on a steel-string guitar without using fingernails - only flesh contact with the strings. When listening to the recording, you might notice some rhythmical changes to the written scores - don't worry, I find it impossible to play a piece the same way twice, and if this lends a slightly improvisatory feel to some of the performances, so much the better. Rather than notate exactly what I played, it is better for you to realise that I am not just playing the dots, and that there is some freedom in these pieces for you to express yourself. I have tried to restrict my changes to the absolute minimum. Feel free to 'do your own thing'.

About the Book

This book was brought into existence by the demands of many of my students (privately and in workshops) who had worked through my previous related book: *Scottish Traditional Music for Guitar in DADGAD and Open G Tunings* (Mel Bay, in the USA, and The Hardie Press in Scotland). That book had no accompanying CD recording. This book includes both easier and more difficult pieces than the previous book, as well as a CD recording.

Any questions? Contact Rob MacKillop via my website www.RMguitar.info where I will try to answer your queries, schedule permitting.

Acknowledgement and Thanks

The recording of the accompanying CD and preparation of the manuscript required the input and talents of a several people and I would like to extend my heartfelt thanks to all those involved, in particular, Ian Green of Greentrax recordings (www.greentrax.com), Peter Haigh of Pier House Studios, Edinburgh and Colin McIver for his encouragement and support, and for reviewing and commenting on the text.

Introduction

Welcome to "*The Scottish Guitar*"

One of my chief concerns in this book is to show the stylistic differences between regions of Scotland, and also between periods. Guitars, lutes and citterns have been played in Scotland for almost a thousand years, and have always had a distinctive, contemplative voice. The arrangements in this book unite history with the present. Different areas of Scotland have cultivated different styles. These regional variations are a vital part of Scottish culture, but I fear they are being eroded due to political and economic pressures. In my arrangements, I have tried to reflect the origin of the tunes, with their appropriate ornaments and phrasing. The accompanying CD is essential for a deeper understanding of the subtle art of phrasing, which cannot be found on the printed page alone.

I have spent many years researching and performing the historical traditional music of Scotland, and I feel that has given me an insight into a Scottish tradition of performing traditional music on plucked, fretted string instruments such as guitar, cittern and lute. I have tried in this book to both show that thousand-year tradition for what it is, and to incorporate it into later material, from Gaelic song to traditional airs and dances. My main hope is that this book will raise an awareness amongst guitarists and their audiences of the great heritage the modern guitar can lay claim to, and the unique and distinctive style of Scottish guitar playing. This book (I believe for the first time) attempts to define a uniquely Scottish way of playing the guitar, and it does so not through a dry academic analysis, but through performance – the heart of any musical culture.

Tunings

Experimenting with alternate tunings is nothing new. During the first half of the 17th century, players of the lute (a guitar-like instrument) notated over 30 (!) different tunings. French players especially enjoyed exploring different resonances and sounds, very often writing down sketches of their improvisations in the form of *preludes* which had no bar lines or time values. Eventually all this experimenting resulted in a near-universal new tuning of an open D minor chord. Perhaps the same thing will eventually happen with the so-called Celtic style of guitar playing. If so, the front runner for supremacy in the tuning stakes seems to be the increasingly popular DADGAD. So it is only natural that the first section of the book commences with two preludes in DADGAD tuning.

The French *luthistes* were a major influence on the Scottish *lutars,* whose own manuscripts amount to over 500 pieces in seven different tunings. I have recorded a lot of this Scottish repertoire for lutes on two discs for the Greentrax label (www.greentrax.com). In arranging these pieces for guitar, I have found that (after much experimenting) a tuning of **Open D** (DADF#AD) suits the music best. Therefore all of the Open D pieces in this book are drawn from the 17th-century Scottish lute manuscripts, including the earliest notated version of *Auld Lang Syne* - but not quite the version you might be used to hearing...

One problem with DADGAD and Open D occurs when your fiddler friend chooses to play in the key of C. With a capo in hand, in DADGAD tuning any key from Eb to F# can be accessed just as easily as D. Using **Open G** tuning allows access to keys from G to C#. With two basic tunings, DADGAD and Open G, all keys are accessible. I strongly advise you to invest in a good-quality capo.

Fingerstyle Guitar Technique

There are many books devoted to honing the perfect fingerstyle technique; therefore I restrict myself to just a few basic comments. My previous book *(Scottish Traditional Music arranged for Guitar in DADGAD and OPEN G Tunings* – Mel Bay Editions) goes into technique in some detail.

The key thing is to cultivate a ***natural*** technique, and that means allowing the hands to do what they were designed to do: open and close. It's that simple, yet it is amazing to observe how many obstacles we put in the way of that happening. A ***bad*** technique is easy to describe: the left hand uses too much pressure when pressing the strings down; the right hand pulls up instead of in. Taking one at a time:

The Left Hand

Place any of your left-hand fingers on any string - but don't press the string down yet. Just let it rest on top of the string. Start plucking with the right hand. As the plucking continues, start adding more pressure to the string, pushing it gently towards the fret. When the note starts to sound the way it should - clear and steady - start releasing the pressure. Return to starting position. Now, how much pressure was needed? If your guitar was set up reasonably well, the pressure required to push the string onto the fret is minimal. Try to remember this lesson whenever you are playing. I can guarantee that most of the time you will be using WAY too much pressure! Start each practice routine by doing this very easy exercise.

You must teach your brain to <u>allow</u> your muscles to work efficiently.

The Right Hand

Place the right-hand thumb on the fifth string and the index, middle and ring fingers on the top three strings. Place the LEFT HAND index finger gently onto the middle joint of the RIGHT HAND index finger. Pluck the string with the right-hand index finger. Did the right-hand index finger move away from the left-hand index finger, or did it push up and into it? The correct movement is away from the left-hand finger. Work at it every day.

You must teach your brain to <u>allow</u> your muscles to do what they were designed to do!

Interpretation

At its most basic, music can be split into three easily identifiable parts:

Melody   Harmony   Rhythm

As you work on a new piece, try to focus on each of these separately, before putting them all together.

Melody

For me, melody is everything. The greatest single influence on my playing is the phrasing of traditional singers, where every phrase is generated by the breath. The melodies included in this book have been chosen for their subtle nuances, which cannot be forced into a metronomic rhythm, and in my performances you will hopefully feel the internal flow of the melody rather than the external pulse of the beat. In other words, there are places where it is difficult to tap your foot in time to the phrasing. I make no apologies for this. On the other hand, this is not an excuse for bad time keeping. Learn to sing the tunes, physically sing them out loud. Then play them on the guitar. If there is a difference, then you are not playing with the phrasing of a singer. The best players "make the instrument sing".

Harmony

Very often with Celtic-style melodies the harmony is ambiguous. **This is one of its strengths.** Too often in the past 300 years, Scottish tunes have been forced into so-called 'correct' harmonies by editors who have been embarrassed by the 'anomalies' in the native air. The most characteristic Scottish melodies stem from medieval modal aesthetics, and do not sit happily in the modern (albeit 400 year old!) major/minor system of tonality. As a result, some terrible crimes have been paid to Scottish melodies over the generations. As Robert Burns said in a complaint to his publisher, Thompson: '...let our National Music preserve its native features. They are, I own, frequently *wild and unreducible to the more modern rules; but on that very eccentricity, perhaps, depends a great part of their effect'*. The phrase 'more modern rules' alludes to the modern harmonic system. I have tried to avoid reducing the wild melodies to this modern system, and sometimes let the melodies sing without any accompaniment at all.

Rhythm

Some of the pieces included here are of a very definite dance rhythm, and it is wise in such instances to tighten-up the rhythm somewhat. Other pieces, however, can be rhythmically very free. Use the recordings as a guide only. You must find your own way of articulating the rhythm of the phrases. Rhythm is an extraordinarily subtle thing, and you should be aware of at least two levels of its influence. The *outer* rhythm, as I call it, is characterized by the beat, usually the downbeat (the first beat) of each bar. The *inner* rhythm is less obvious and harder to discuss with words, yet is arguably more important. Again, it is governed by the breath. We do not breathe metronomically, even when dancing, so why should we when we are playing? Have you ever noticed that you have a quick intake of breath when a new idea suddenly enters your head? Each phrase is a new idea, or a consequence of one.

Summary: Melody, Harmony, Rhythm - it's all the same. Let it breathe!

Ornamentation

I have not written out the ornaments I use, for the following reasons:
a) I am very often not conscious that I am playing an ornament
b) Each time I play a piece I play it differently, using similar ornaments but in different places
c) If an ornament is written out, the student tends to play it exactly the same way, in the same place each time. It is better to show you the *types* of ornaments I use; so that you can add them wherever you feel moved to do so
d) The study of ornaments is a red herring. It's all about breathing phrases (there I go again!)

My previous DADGAD book (see *Introduction*) goes into much greater detail, so here I will just give a quick outline of the ornaments I use.

Lower mordant: after playing a melody note, quickly alternate it with a note on the same string below the melody note. Very often this will mean pulling off to an open string. And then quickly play the original note again. So three notes are sounded very quickly.

Upper mordant: as above, but alternate with a note above the melody note.

Trill: rapidly alternate two notes as many times as feels right

Cross-string trill: play the two notes of a trill on adjacent strings

Tremolo: listen to the B section of *Lilt - Milne*. Here I use tremolos on some of the melody notes. It is really a very fast striking of the melody note with thumb, ring finger, middle finger and finally index finger.

Section 1: Tunes in DADGAD Tuning

A Word About DADGAD Tuning

The great thing about DADGAD tuning is how good it makes the average player sound. Despite our worst efforts, it is difficult to sound bad in DADGAD. It is the perfect tuning for *noodling* - just letting your fingers go for a walk on the fretboard. Italian musicians of the 16th century called such pieces, *Toccatas* - from the verb 'to touch'. Later the term, *Prelude* became more common, as players would improvise passages while checking the tuning of their instrument before playing a more structured piece.

So I've started with two improvised preludes. The first introduces a simple melody against simple but interesting harmonies, the type often favoured by DADGAD players. The second prelude explores some of the unusual chords that DADGAD offers players. Have fun exploring these chords, and use different right-hand patterns, or strum as explored in the recording on the repeat of the whole piece.

DADGAD is the name spelled out by the open strings of the guitar in what has become the most common tuning for Celtic fingerstyle-guitar playing. Compared to standard tuning (EADGBE) the 5th, 4th and 3rd strings remain the same, whilst the other strings are all tuned downwards by one tone. This downward tuning relaxes the tension of the instrument, and this seems to suit the style of music particularly well.

Track 1: Prelude No.1 (Rob MacKillop)

This short piece can be heard on TRACK 1 of the CD. It is designed to introduce the drone quality of the open strings against a simple melody. Try to let all the notes ring on as long as possible. The pace is slow. Listen to the sound of the intervals, the different notes, as they clash against or complement each other. Later, try improvising your own similar melodies surrounded by the warm drone of the open strings. The piece ends with a scale played across the strings in a technique known as *campanella* - think of bell ringing. This technique is used extensively in Celtic guitar fingerstyle playing.

Track 2: Prelude No.2 (Rob MacKillop)

This piece introduces some of the unusual chords used by DADGAD players. There is little point in working out new fingerings for standard chords such as G and A - might as well use standard tuning for such boring old sounds. DADGAD offers the chance to play such atmospheric chords as Gadd9 and AMajor3sus4. Having said that, most players still refer to these chords as G and A!

There are no barlines in the following piece and no time signals, so play as freely as possible and enjoy the unique chordal sounds of DADGAD tuning. Try different right-hand picking patterns or even try strumming. Advanced players might want to experiment with improvising single-note solos over this chordal outline.

Notes to the Tunes

Phiurag nan Gaol - Sister of Loves
Just the open sixth string is used here to accompany the melody. The jump from the last note of bar 3 to the first note of bar 4 is deliberate, if awkward. By playing the first note of bar 4 on the *third* string, the passage would be easier to play, technically speaking, but the phrasing would come out wrong. Sometimes these large intervals require large physical leaps with our hands in order for them to sing well.

Tighean Geala Sildeag
A Gaelic dance, but don't be too strict with the pulse.

Oran a' Mhaighdean Mhara
The first four notes are a guitar cliché. Note the C natural in bar 6 (last note), indicating the mixolydian mode.

Low Lies The Mist on Mallavurich
I included the original bass line supplied in Patrick MacDonald's Collection as an example of the classical bass lines that were creeping into Gaelic music in the 18th century, but this one is not too bad and gives you a good exercise in playing two voices. (Capo on 2nd fret)

Maol Donaidh - The Fisherman's Song for Attracting the Seals
A gentle jig that requires no harmony, especially when set out across the guitar strings instead of along them. Keep this in mind when arranging your own jigs and reels. (Capo on 2nd fret)

Suas Leis a' Mhagairlean
This reel can tolerate many different speeds. Remember that slurs (pull-offs and hammer-ons) should have a strong first note and a weaker second. This sounds more rhythmical. (Capo on 2nd fret)

My Cheeks are Furrowed
The piece starts with a slide from the fourth fret to the seventh on the first string. Try not to allow the intervening notes of the slide to sound too clearly. Slides can be beautiful as well as horrible!

Farewell to whisky
This can be played fairly slow as well as fairly fast, depending on your mood (and technique!). Of course, it should always be played before the next piece.

Welcome Whisky Back Again
I have set this low on the guitar on the first page, and high on the second page. You can play both or choose one only. Both these Neil Gow tunes were originally published with great rhythmical precision, but traditionally both are played with some amount of freedom.

Roslin Castle
DADGAD can be useful for tunes in B minor. There is some debate over whether James Oswald wrote this piece. Whoever did, deserves our thanks.

The Flooers O' the Forest
The great anti-war ballad, again arranged in two octave settings. Play one or both. This is a much more ornamented version than that which appeared in my previous DADGAD book (see *Introduction*).

Phiurag nan gaol - Sister of loves

arr.Rob MacKillop

Patrick McDonald Collection

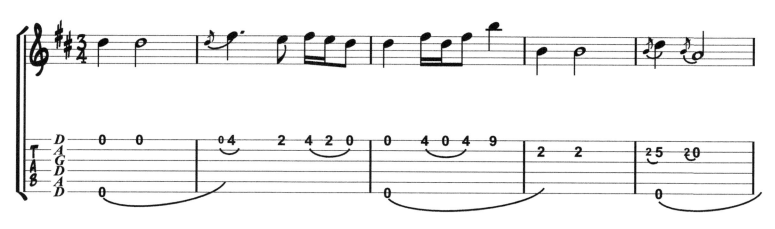

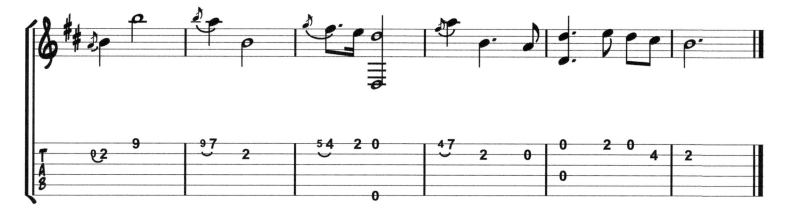

Tighean Geala Sildeag

Arr.Rob MacKillop

Traditional

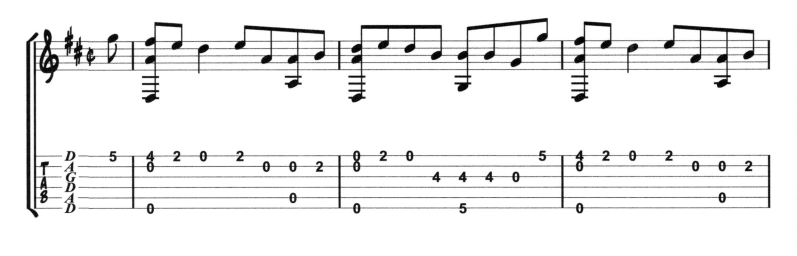

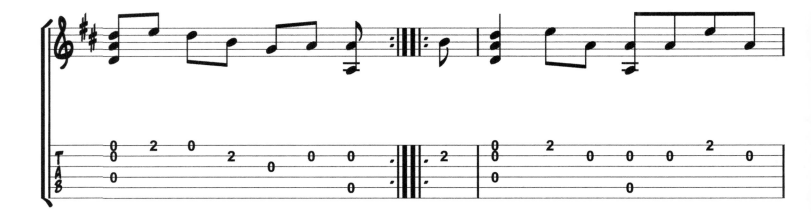

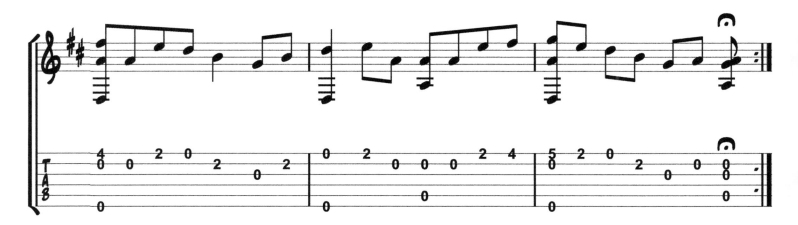

Oran a' Mhaighdean Mhara

ARR.Rob MacKillop

Traditional

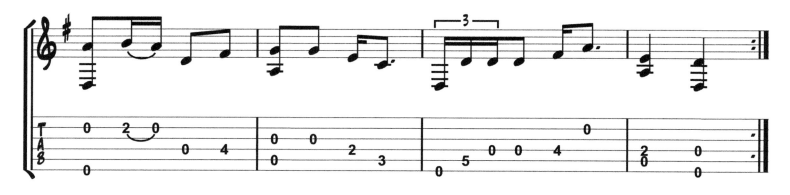

Low lies the mist on Mallavurich

arr.Rob MacKillop

Patrick MacDonald Collection

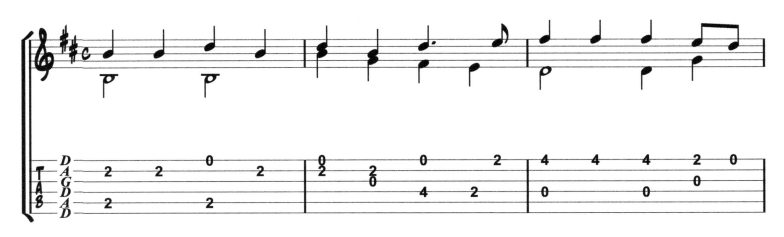

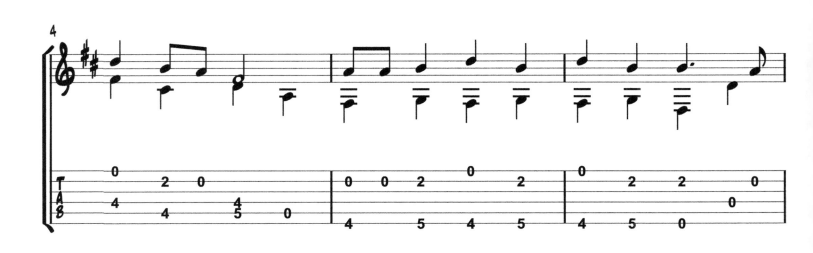

Maol donaidh - The fisherman's song for attracting the seals

arr.Rob MacKillop

Patrick MacDonald Collection

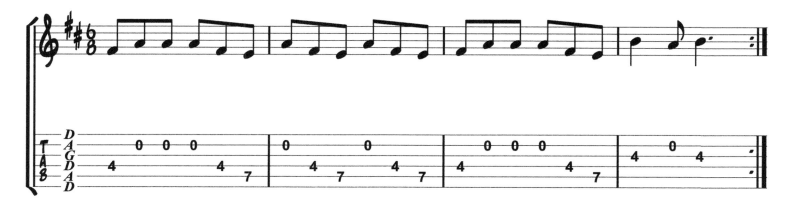

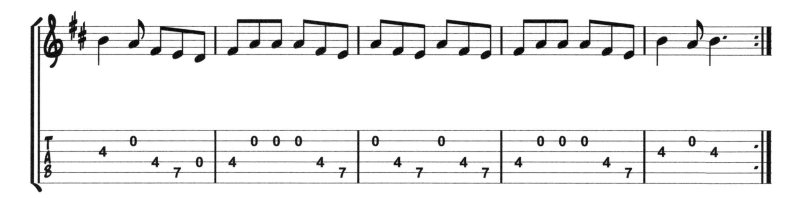

Suas Leis a' Mhagairlean

Arr. Rob MacKillop

Traditional

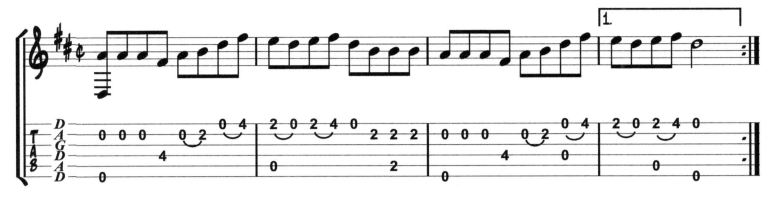

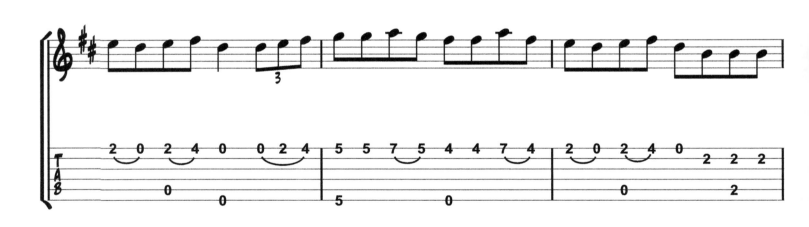

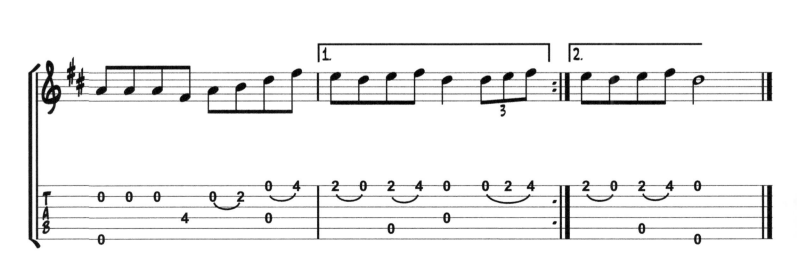

My Cheeks Are Furrowed

Arr.Rob MacKillop

Patrick MacDonald Collection

Farewell To Whisky

arr. Rob MacKillop

Niel Gow

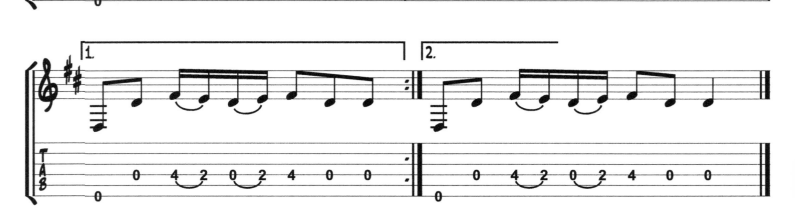

Welcome Whisky Back Again

Arr. Rob MacKillop

Niel Gow

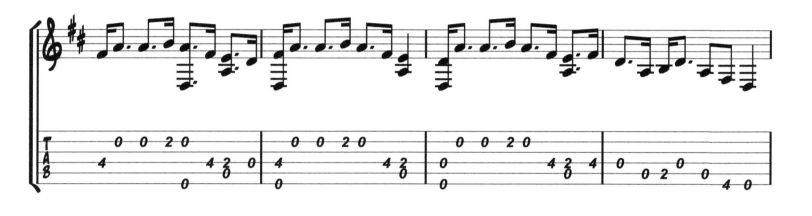

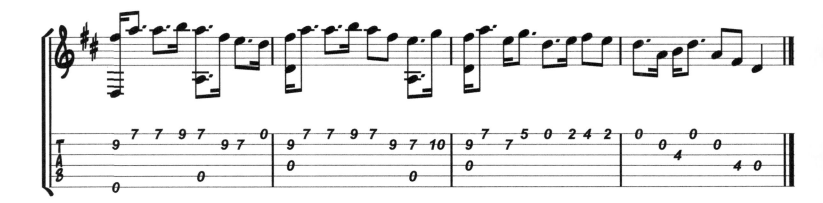

Roslin Castle

arr. Rob MacKillop

James Oswald

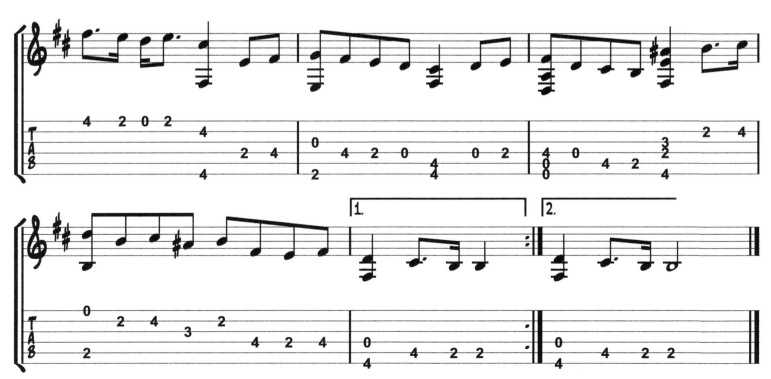

The Flooers O The Forest

Arr. Rob MacKillop

Traditional

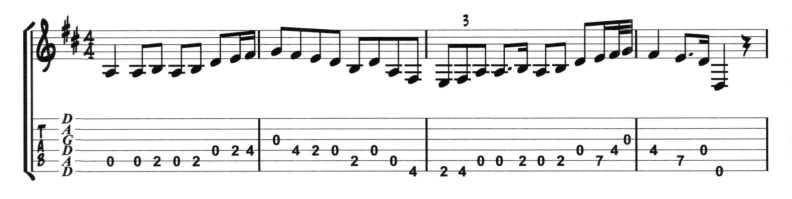

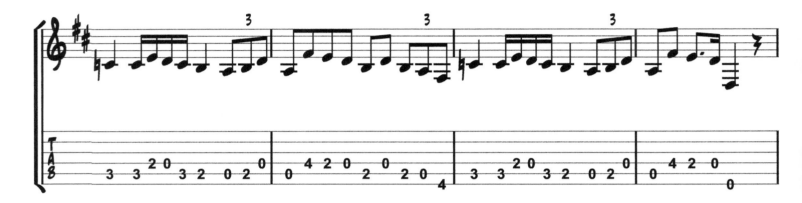

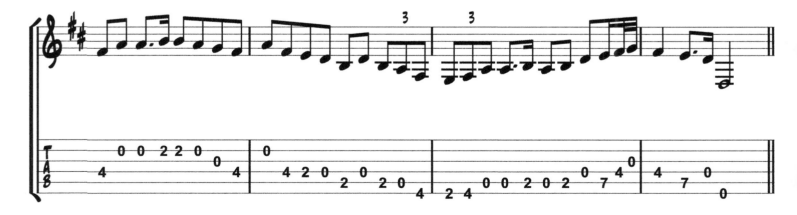

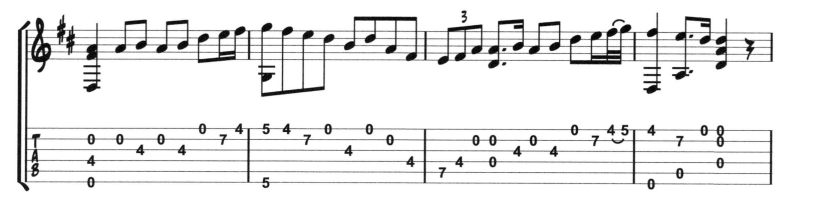

Section 2: Tunes in Open G Tuning

A Word About Open G Tuning

I first encountered Open G tuning through the playing of Keith Richards of The Rolling Stones, and it is very popular with blues slide guitar players, ancient and modern. But it is also very useful for Celtic-style guitar players. The strings are tuned (from the bass upwards): DGDGBD - lots of tonic (G) and dominant (D) drone notes.

Notes to the Tunes

Wet is the Night and Cold

Requires only the minimum of harmony. Concentrate on phrasing the melody, and learn to sing it. Once familiar, try adding ornaments and variations.

A Mother's Lament on the Death of Her Child

Robert Burns put words to this ancient Gaelic air. Slow, steady and serious...

Gur Eutrom an t Aiseag

Although the tune was originally written down with great rhythmical care, do not worry too much about the timing. The feeling is more important. (Capo on 2nd fret)

An Chearc ar fad is an Anairthe

Not too fast, not too slow, the rhythm should be quite steady. (Capo on 2nd fret)

Ask my father

Notice the cross-string trill in bar two, beat 10. If this proves too tricky, just leave it out and little harm will be done. (Capo on 2nd fret)

My Love Has Deceived Me

A slow waltz? This was notated before the waltz took a hold in Scotland, so don't be too tempted to play it in strict waltz style.

Oran an Aoig - The Song of Death

One of my favourite of Burns's borrowed airs. Again, not much harmony, so spend your time carefully shaping the melody.

Wet is the Night and Cold

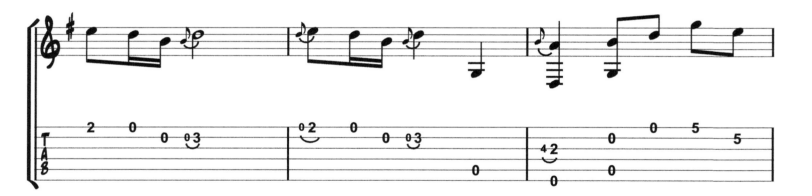

A MOTHER'S LAMENT ON THE DEATH OF HER CHILD

ARR.ROB MACKILLOP

PATRICK MACDONALD COLLECTION

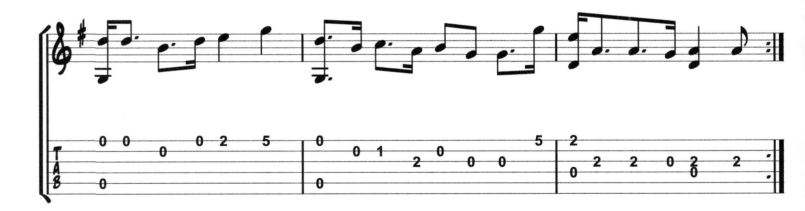

Gur eutrom an t aiseag

Arr.Rob MacKillop

Patrick MacDonald Collection

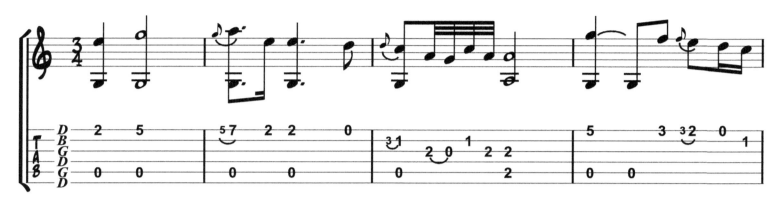

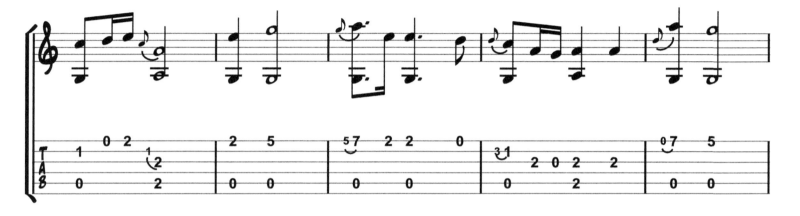

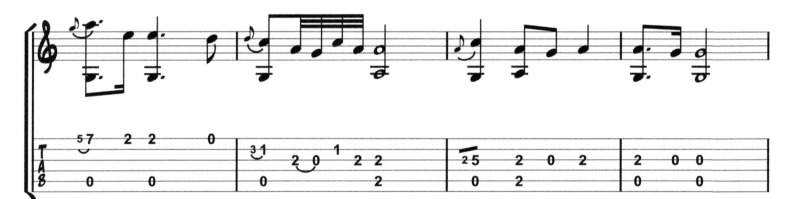

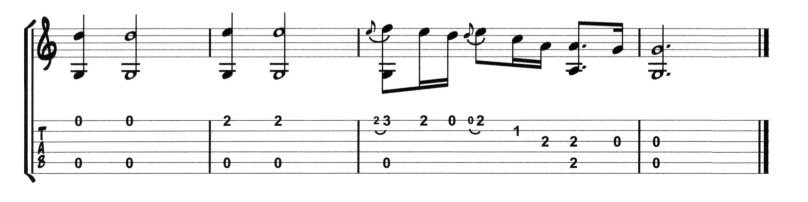

AN CHEARC AR FAD IS AN ANAIRTHE

TRADITIONAL

Ask My Father

ARR. Rob MacKillop

Traditional

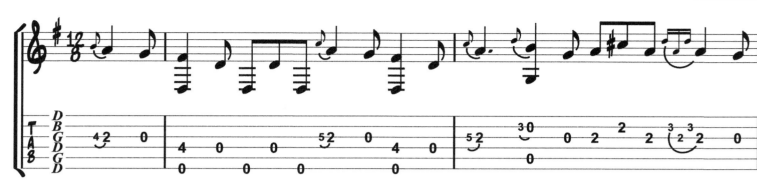

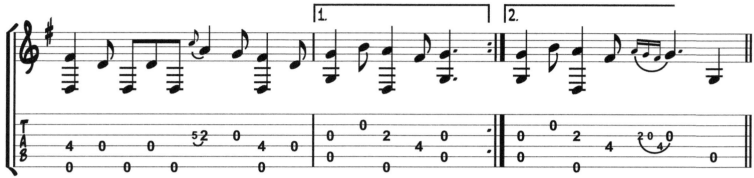

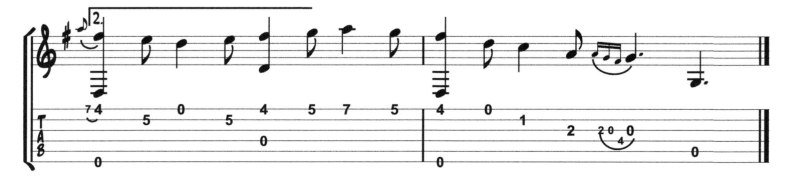

My love has deceived me

arr. Rob MacKillop

Patrick MacDonald Collection

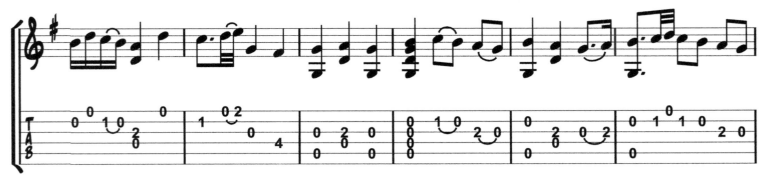

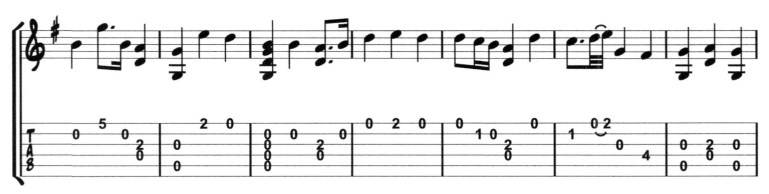

Oran an aoig – The Song of Death

Patrick MacDonald Collection

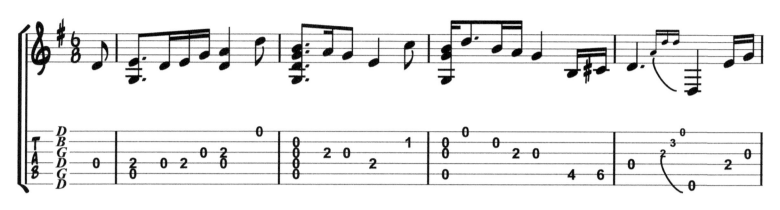

Copyright © RMP 2004

Section 3: Tunes in Open D Tuning

A Word About Open D Tuning

This section of the book is dedicated to my transcriptions of the Scottish lute repertoire of the 17th century. As you will hear, Scottish musicians had as individual a style of playing Scottish music on the lute as they were to have playing Scottish music on the Italian violin - they adapted it to their own tastes. So when you think of the lute, banish all thoughts of Henry VIII, damsels in distress and balcony love scenes! The Scottish lute world is very different indeed.

There are over 500 pieces in Scottish lute manuscripts, all of which survive from the 17th century alone. This was not a new fad, however, as the lute had already been in Scotland for 400 years. There is plenty of evidence that the lute was known and loved in all corners of Scotland (Gaelic as well as Scots) since the medieval period. The religious Reformation of 1560 caused many instruments and manuscripts to be burned, which goes some way to explaining the absence of manuscripts from pre 1600. And, of course, much of the music was never written down in the first place. So we are lucky that so much does survive from the 17th century, and we are particularly lucky that most of what survives is high quality traditional music. Here can be found the roots of the roots of Scottish traditional music...

You can hear my recording of many of these pieces on the lute on my Greentrax recordings (www.greentrax.com).

The tuning of the guitar is (from bass to treble) DADF#AD. From DADGAD, just lower the third string by one semitone.

Notes to the Tunes

I Long For Thy Virginitie
I play this very freely. Bar 9 is a little odd, but somehow works.

Rhona's Tune
This is originally untitled, but I have named it after my daughter. You can call it whatever you like! The C section is my own variation.

Shoes Rare and Good In All - Lilt Ladie An Gordoun
The 'shoes' of the title might mean 'She is'. I added the variation, but it is only a repeat of the B section an octave higher.

The Canaries
Great fun to play and a winner in concerts. Take your time with this one; it is well worth the effort.

Lady Lie Near Me
One of the few original tunes to have three sections. [Capo on 2nd fret]

Lilt-Milne
This melody soars for over two octaves. Try singing that distance. Notice how much energy is needed. You must find some way to duplicate that in your playing. (Capo on 2nd fret)

My Lady Binnis Lilt
A wee gem. I could wax lyrically about the B section for many hours. Check out the harmony, rhythm and the sudden appearance of the mixolydian mode. A miniature masterpiece. (Capo on 2nd fret)

Blew Riben
A tricky piece but great fun. (Capo on 2nd fret)

Lady Lothian's Lilt
This tune appears in quite a few manuscripts and seems to have been a favourite. Each time it appears there are many differences, which indicates that a culture of improvisation was alive and well. It also tells us that we can be quite free in our own interpretations. (Capo on 2nd fret)

Courante and Double
The courante was a popular dance in the 17th century. The 'double' refers to a decoration of the same piece using running quavers. This piece displays the perfect wedding of French and Scottish styles. When played on the lute, it is a case of the Auld Alliance on the Auld Appliance! There are wide stretches for the left hand, so a capo is advisable. (Capo on 2nd fret)

A Port (No.1)
The first of six *ports* (Gaelic: tune/air). These pieces are full of subtle shifts and shades. There is nothing else in world musical culture that sounds remotely like these pieces.

A Port (No.2)
A *classic* port: note the rising octaves at the beginning and the falling octaves at the end - indicating a tuning prelude. All of the Wemyss manuscript ports share, in more or less subtle ways, this form.

Port Jean Lindsay
A perfect blend of tuning prelude and Gaelic air.

Port Priest
Two contrasting sections played AABBA.

Port Rorie Dall
Was this really a composition by the blind itinerant Irish harper on a trip to Scotland?

Port Atholl
This port from the Balcarres manuscript reveals how the port developed over the 50 years since the Wemyss ports. The classic traits are still there but are far less obvious. One of my favourite pieces.

The Chancellours Farewell
The Balcarres pieces all show a development of the bass line, a Baroque influence, and also introduce variations. [Capo on 2nd fret]

If Thou Were Myn Own Thing
The rhythm of the A section is quite abstract, especially as the melody (known from other sources) is quite flowing. This is a fairly avant-garde arrangement for the period.

The Lord Aboin's Air
A beautiful air, with fine variations.

For Old Long Syne
This was notated almost 100 years before the Robert Burns's version. A few traditional singers have resurrected the Burns version in recent years, and the Balcarres version has some phrases in common with it, and some that are entirely different. Not only is this the earliest notated version, but it also comes with variations and harmony. Note that it starts on a minor chord...

I Long For Thy Virginitie

Arr. Rob MacKillop

Straloch MS

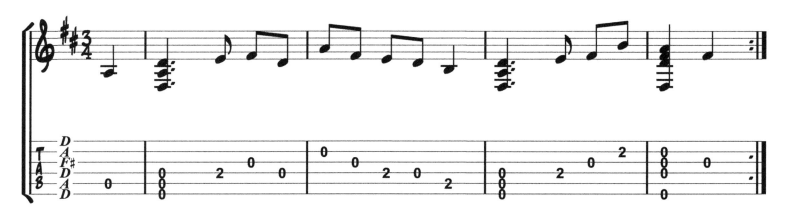

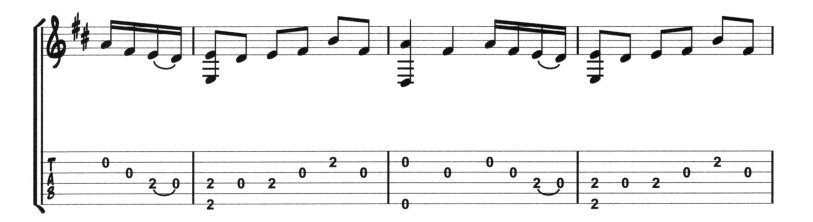

Rhona's Tune

arr. Rob MacKillop

Rowallan MS

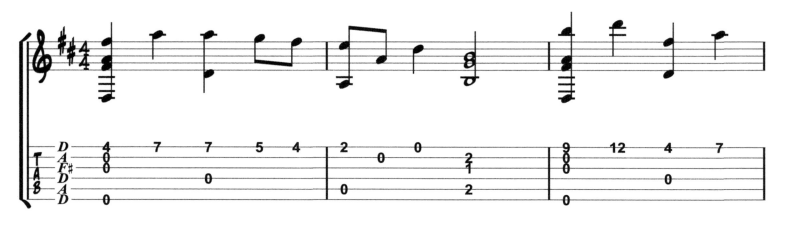

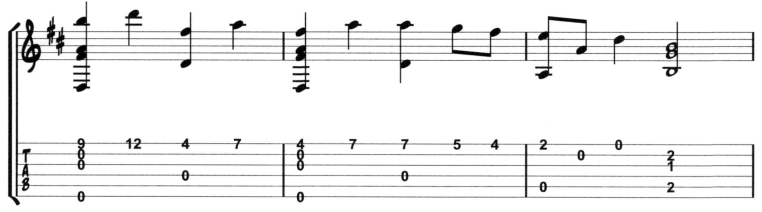

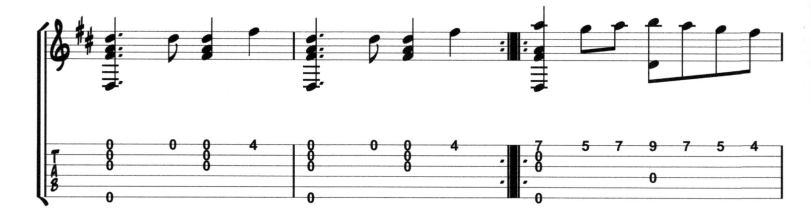

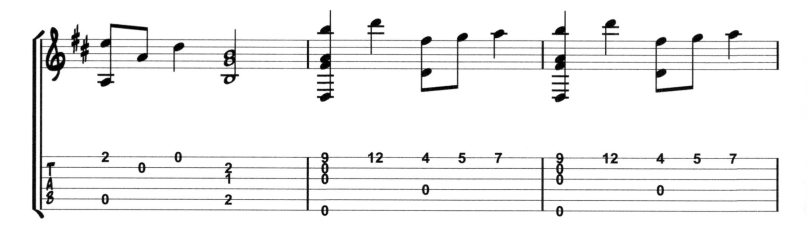

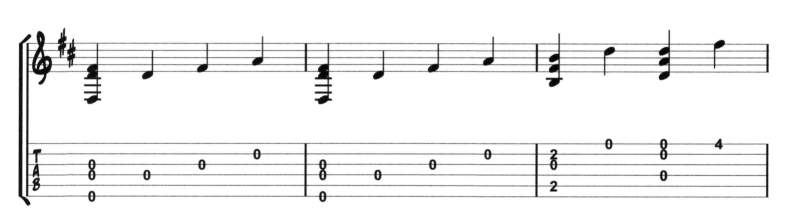

Shoes Rare and Good in All – Lilt Ladie An Gordoun

arr.Rob MacKillop

Straloch MS

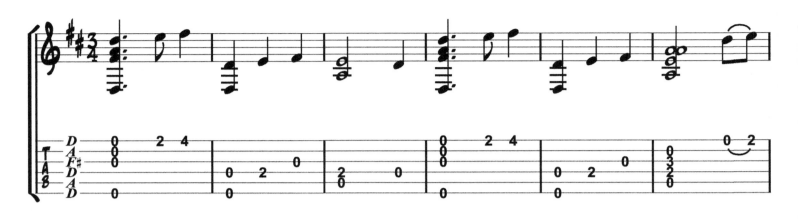

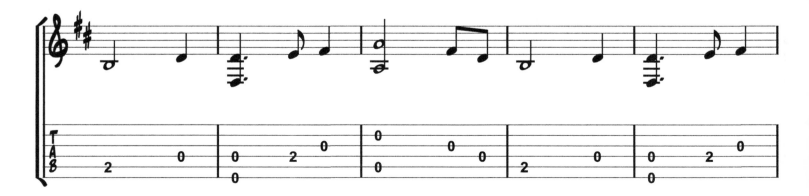

Variation

The Canaries

arr. Rob MacKillop

Straloch MS

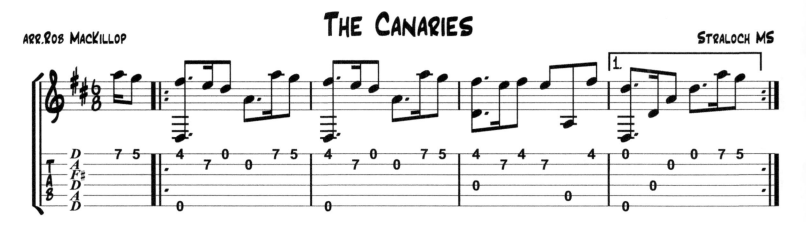

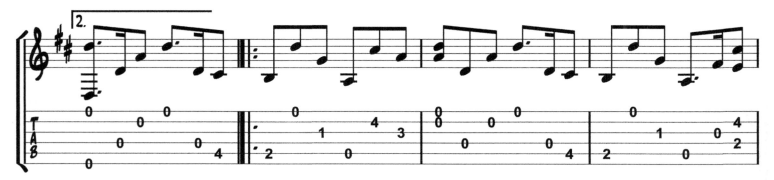

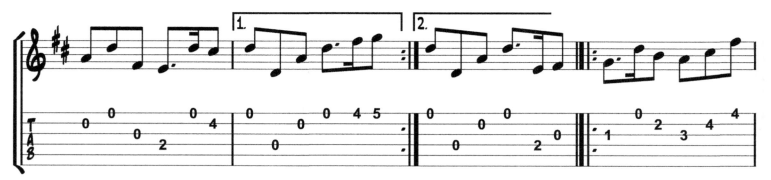

Lady Lie Near Me

arr. Rob MacKillop

Wemyss MS

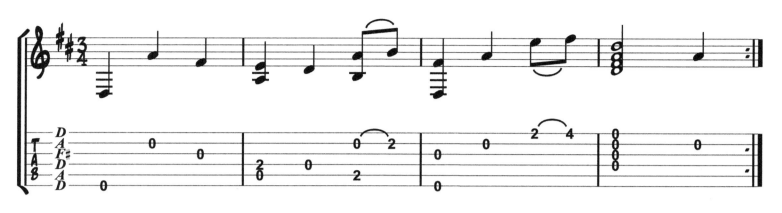

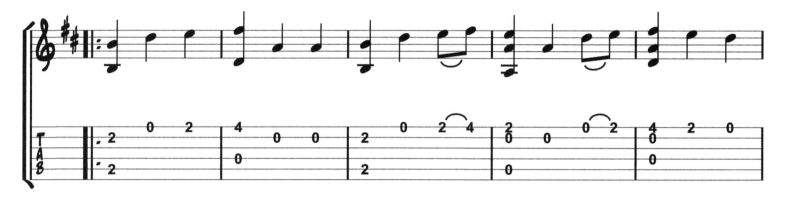

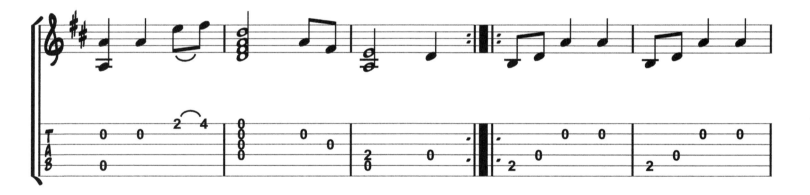

Lilt-Milne

arr. Rob MacKillop

Wemyss MS

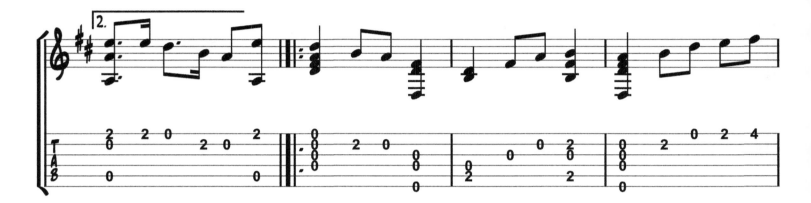

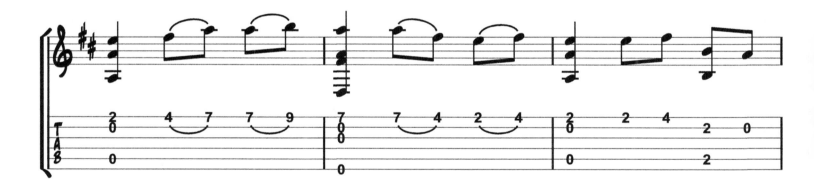

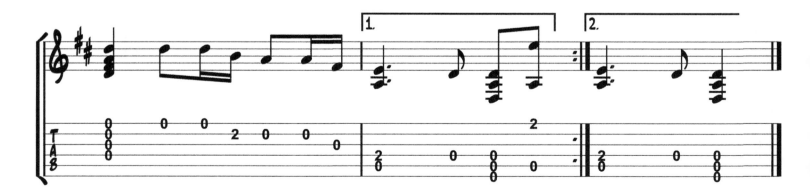

My Lady Binnis Lilt

ARR.ROB MACKILLOP

WEMYSS MS

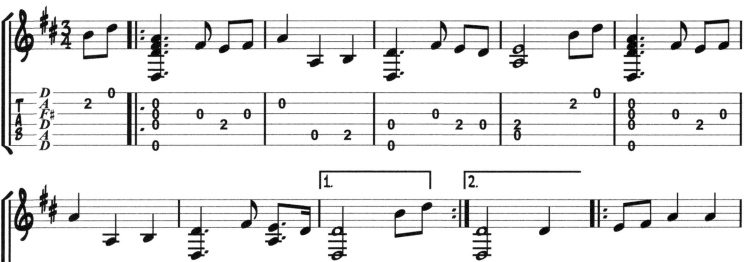

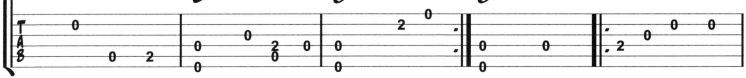

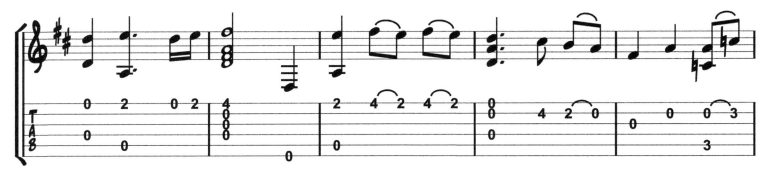

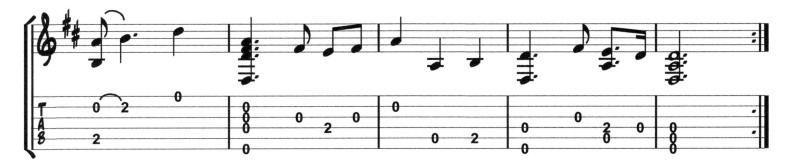

Blew Riben

arr. Rob MacKillop

Wemyss MS

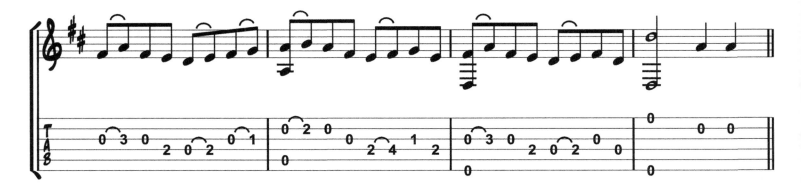

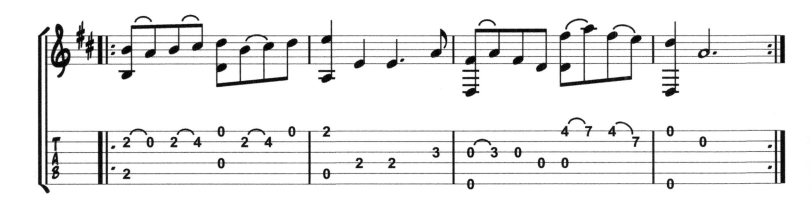

Lady Lothian's Lilt

arr.Rob MacKillop

Panmure 5 MS

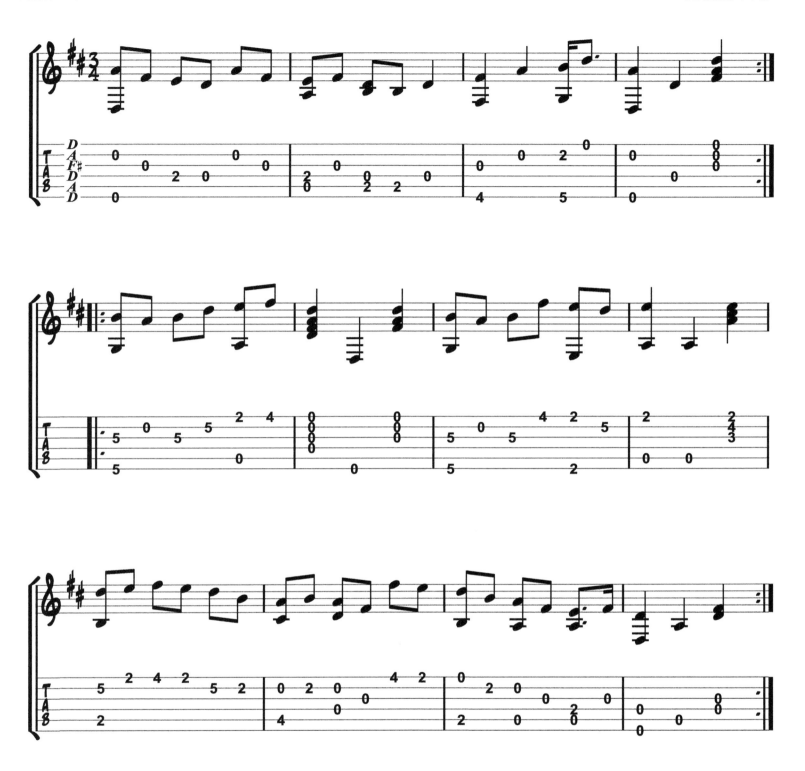

Copyright © RMP 2004

arr.Rob MacKillop

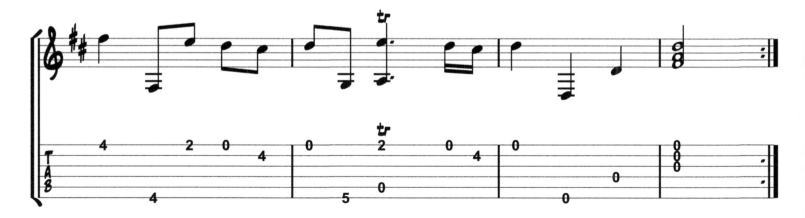

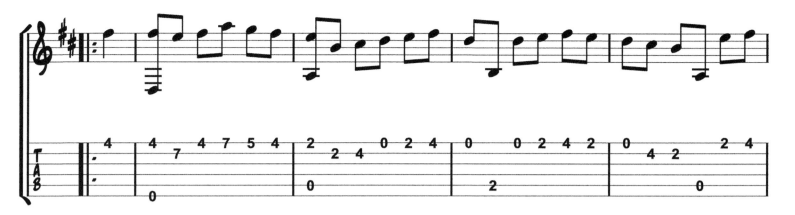

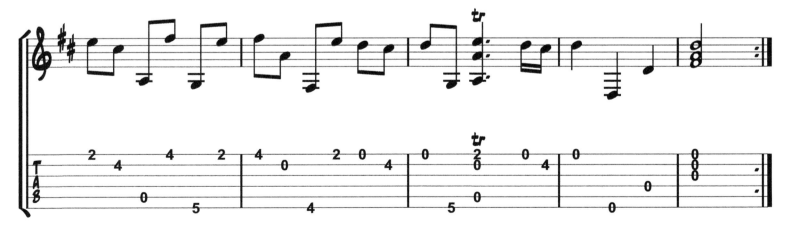

A Port (No.1)

arr. Rob MacKillop

Straloch MS

50

A Port (No.2)

Arr. Rob MacKillop

Straloch MS

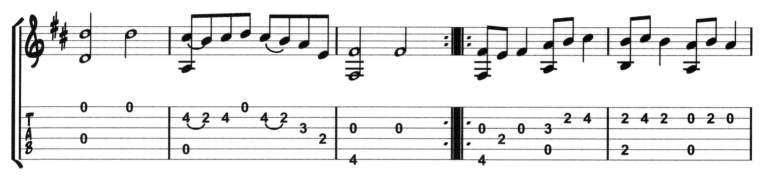

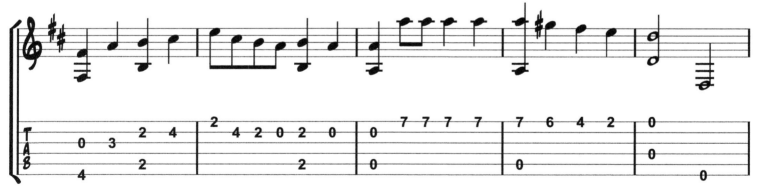

Port Jean Lindsay

arr. Rob MacKillop

Straloch MS

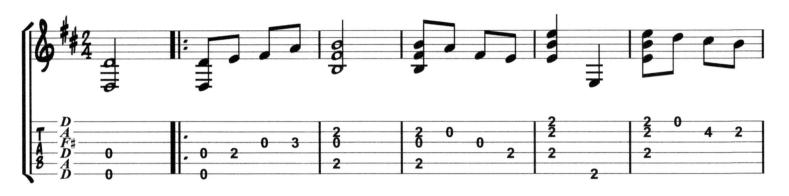

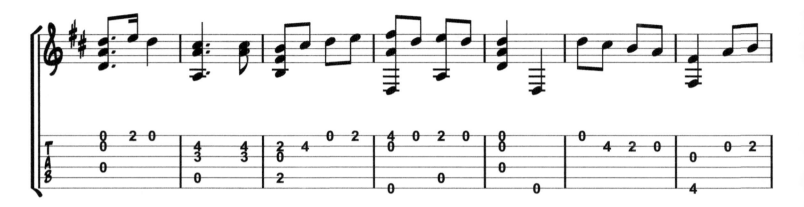

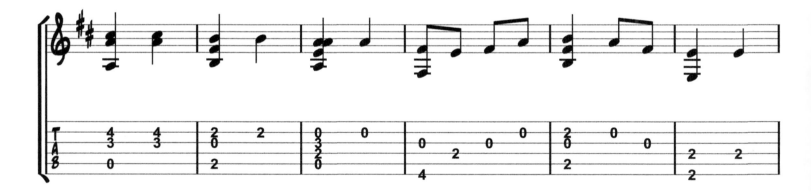

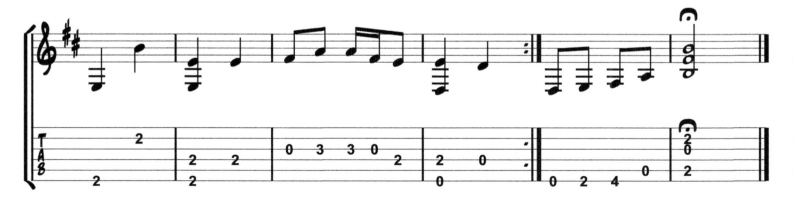

Port Priest

Arr.Rob MacKillop

Straloch MS

Port Rorie Dall

arr. Rob MacKillop

Straloch MS

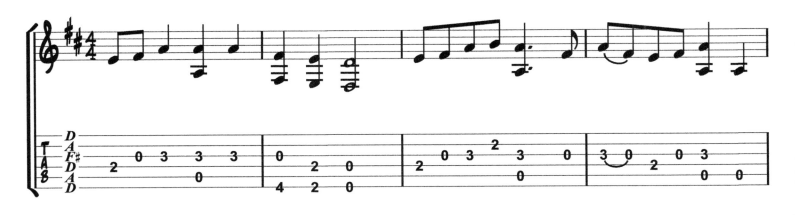

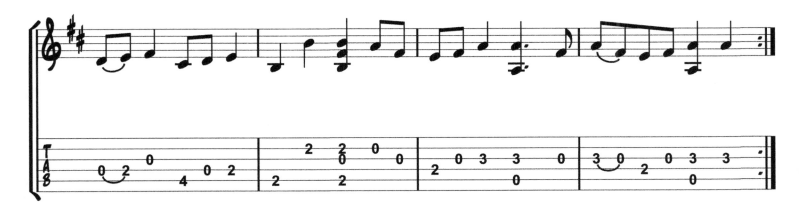

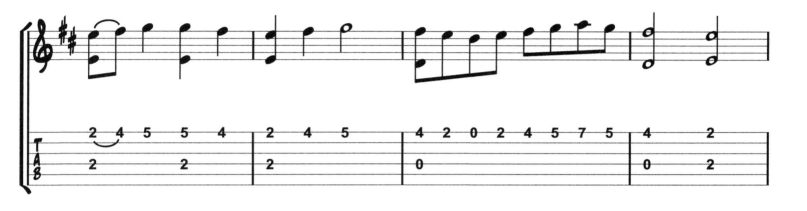

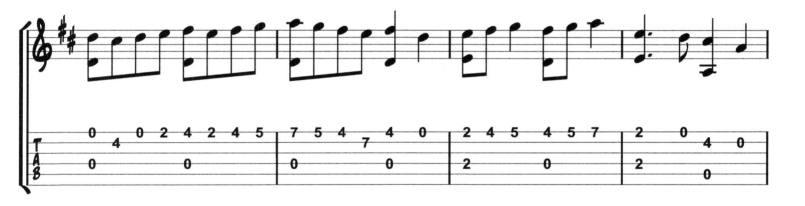

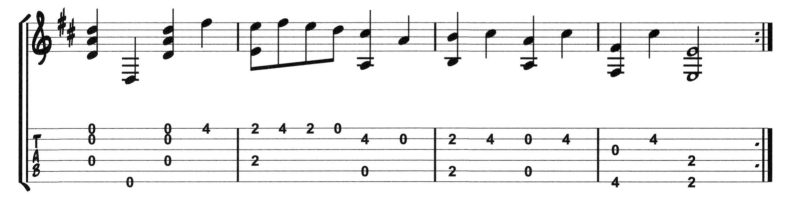

Port Atholl

arr. Rob MacKillop

Balcarres MS

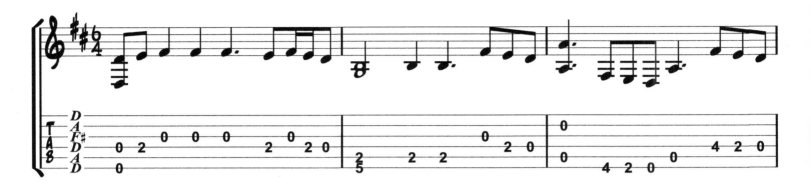

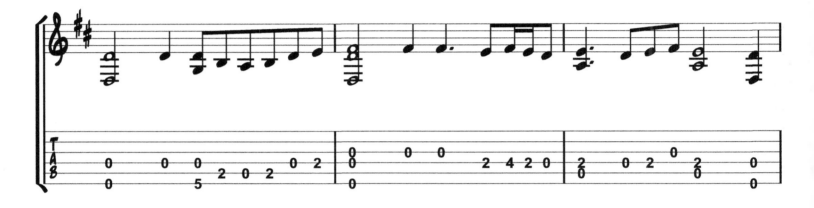

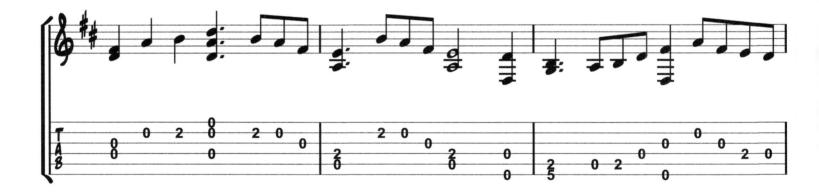

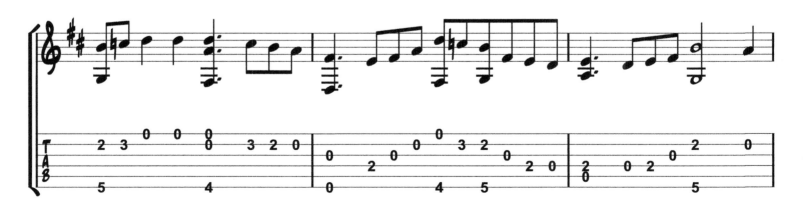

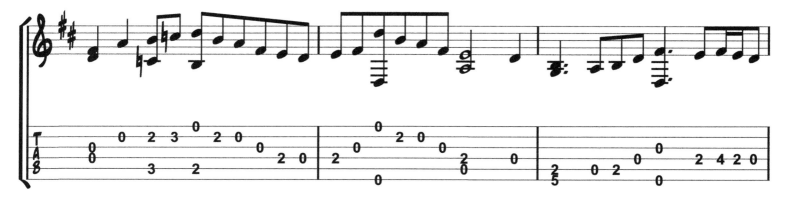

The Chancellours Farewell

arr. Rob MacKillop

Balcarres MS

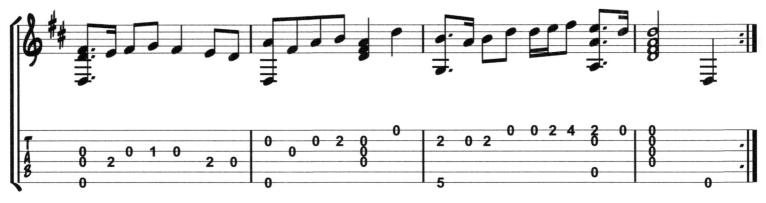

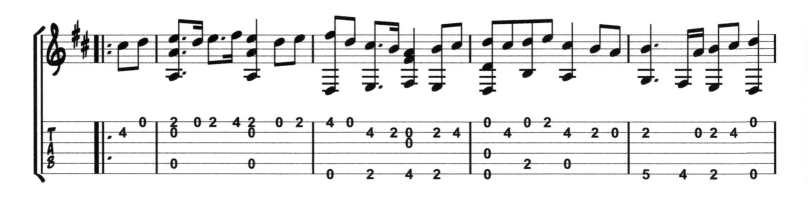

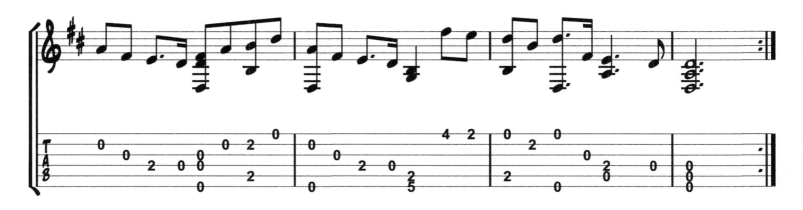

If thou were myn own thing

aRR.Rob MacKillop

Balcarres MS

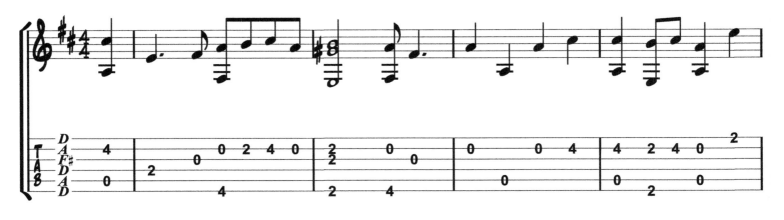

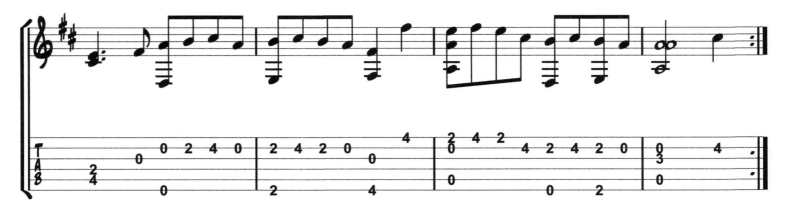

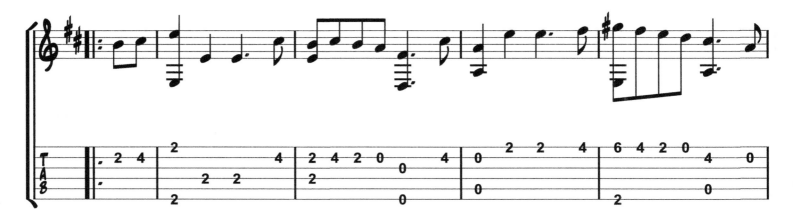

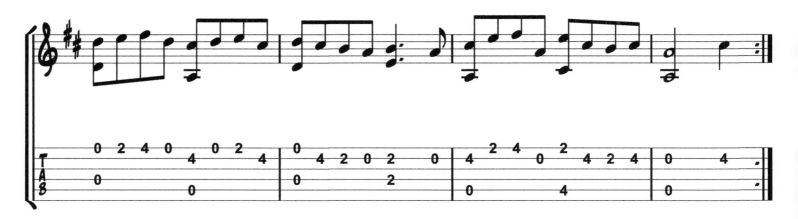

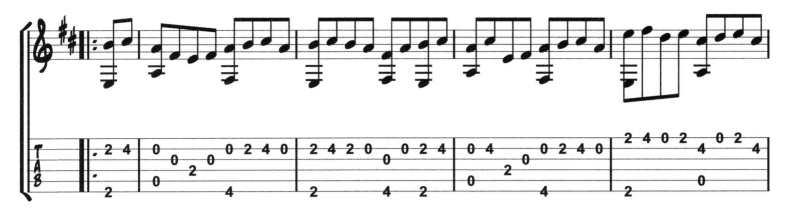

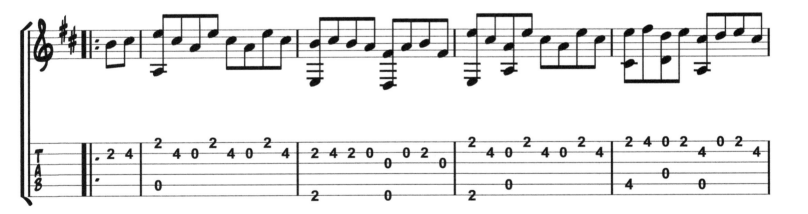

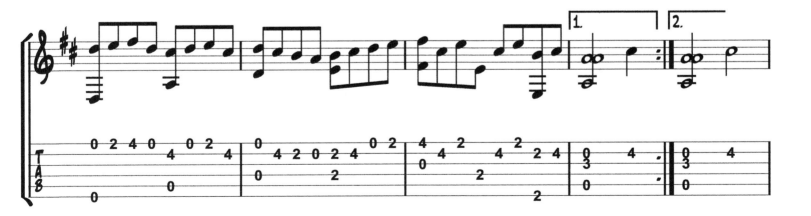

The Lord Aboin's Air

Arr. Rob MacKillop

Balcarres MS

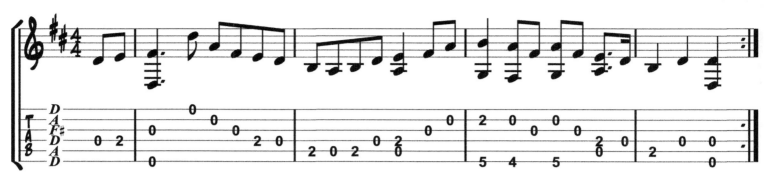

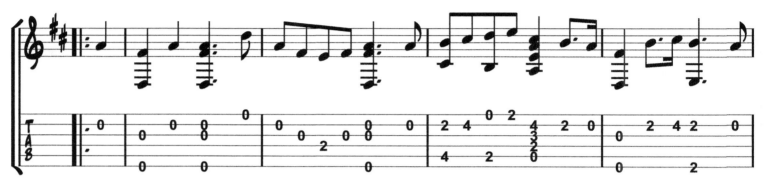

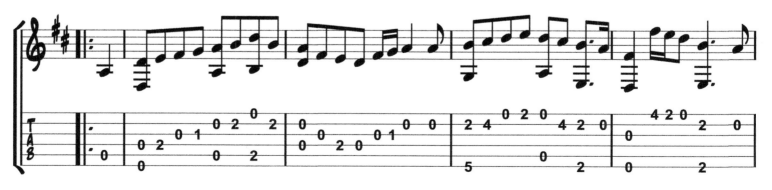

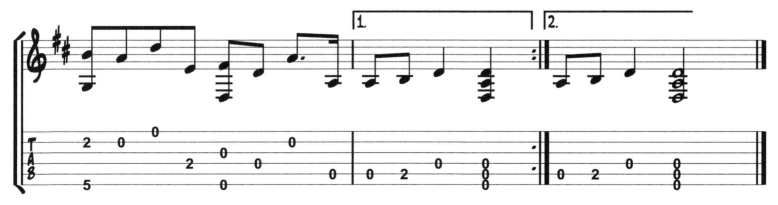

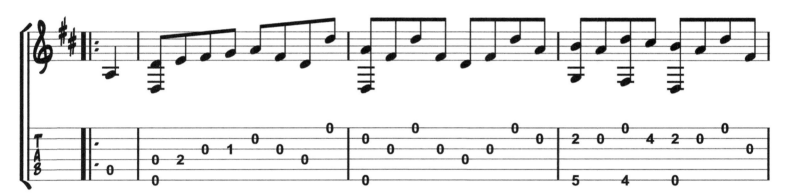

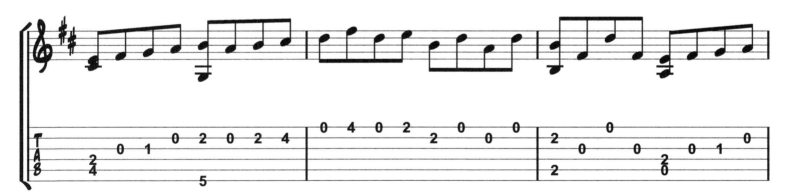

For Old Long Syne

Arr.Rob MacKillop

Balcarres MS

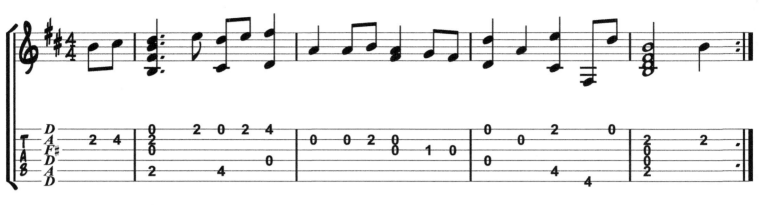

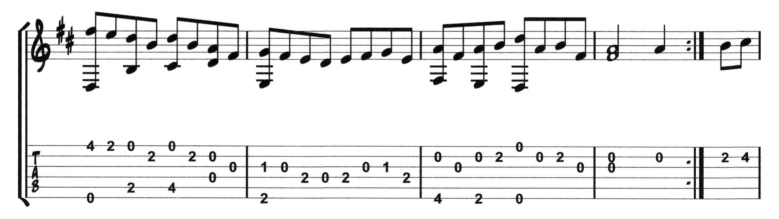

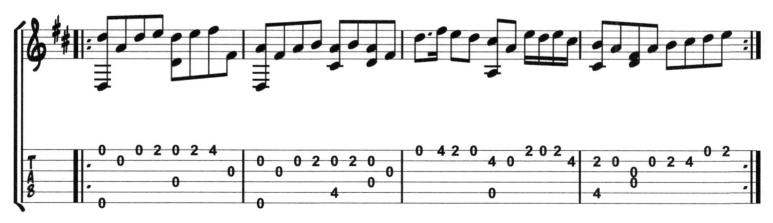

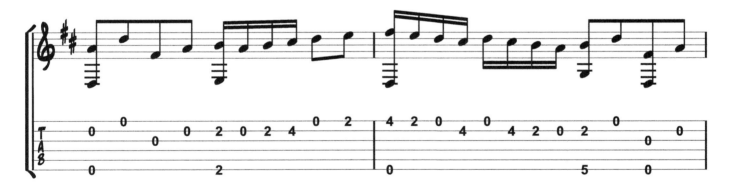
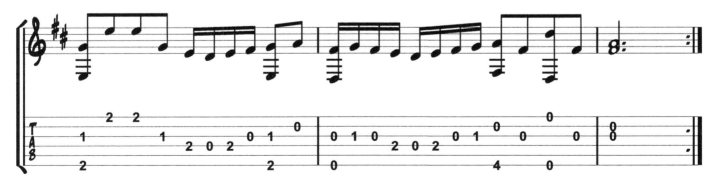

More Great Guitar Books from Centerstream...

More Great Guitar Books from Centerstream...

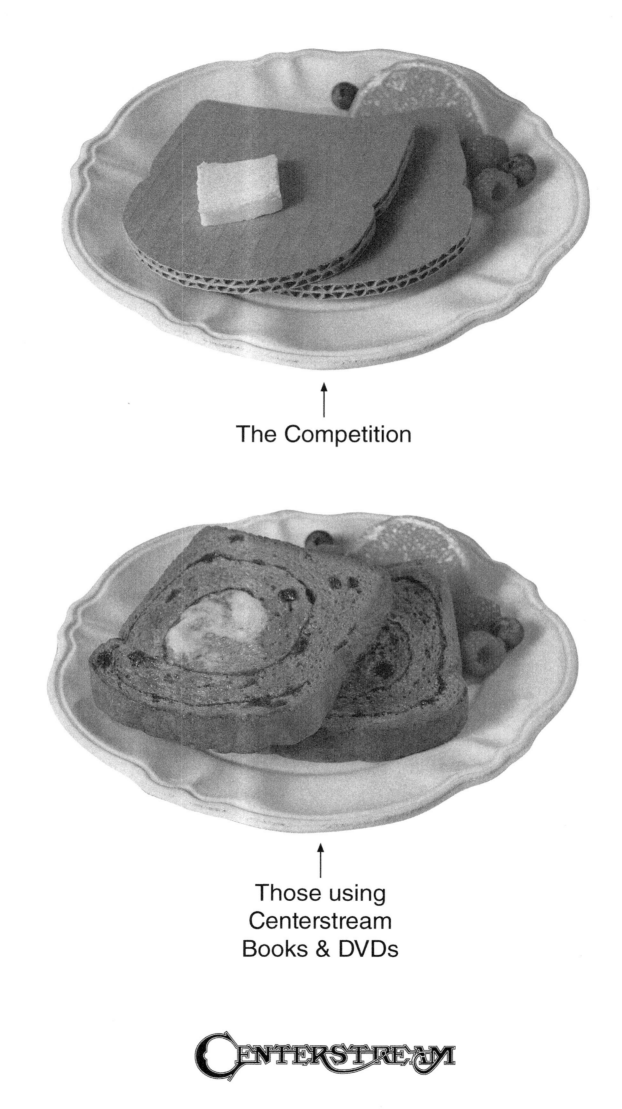

The Competition

Those using
Centerstream
Books & DVDs

CENTERSTREAM